First
Facts®

SUPER SCARY STUFF

SUPER SCARY MONSTERS

BY MEGAN COOLEY PETERSON

Raintree is an imprint of Capstone Global Library Limited, a company incorporated in England and Wales having its registered office at 264 Banbury Road, Oxford, OX2 7DY – Registered company number: 6695582

www.raintree.co.uk
myorders@raintree.co.uk

Text © Capstone Global Library Limited 2017
The moral rights of the proprietor have been asserted.

Edited by Carrie Braulick Sheely
Designed by Kyle Grenz
Picture research by Svetlana Zhurkin
Production by Katy LaVigne
Printed and bound in China

ISBN 978 1 4747 2065 6 (hardback)
20 19 18 17 16
10 9 8 7 6 5 4 3 2 1

ISBN 978 1 4747 2070 0 (paperback)
21 20 19 18 17
10 9 8 7 6 5 4 3 2 1

British Library Cataloguing in Publication Data
A full catalogue record for this book is available from the British Library.

Acknowledgements
We would like to thank the following for permission to reproduce photographs: Dreamstime: Jaime Pharr, 13 (back); Fortean Picture Library: William M. Rebsamen, 7 (left); Getty Images: Ed Vebell, 9 (bottom); iStockphoto: Rich Legg, cover; Shutterstock: Alexlky, 11, DarkBird, 21, Denis Belitsky, 5, Fotokostic, 17, Lukasz Nowak, 9 (top), Neftali, 15 (inset), paintings, 15 (back), Sergey Mironov, 1, Unholy Vault Designs, 7 (right); SuperStock: Pantheon, 13 (inset); Svetlana Zhurkin, 19

Design Elements by Shutterstock

CONTENTS

SCARY MONSTERS ALL AROUND

You're hiking in the woods. A twig snaps nearby. You turn to see a figure darting between the trees. What was it? For thousands of years, people have told monster stories. Some *legendary* creatures feed on blood. Others are half human and half animal. Monsters can be made up. But others may be real. These scary creatures are whispered about in the dark. Are you ready to meet them?

legendary – something based on a story handed down from earlier times; legends are often based on fact, but they may not be entirely true

A FLYING NIGHTMARE

Imagine travelling in a car down a dark road. Suddenly a birdlike creature with glowing red eyes swoops down. You and the monster are face to face.

This monster was first reported near Point Pleasant, West Virginia, USA, in 1966. People nicknamed it the Mothman. Some people say the Mothman is an *alien*. Others believe it's a large bird called a crane.

Creepy cryptids

Some monsters, such as the Mothman, are called *cryptids*. Some people believe these monsters really exist. A few cryptids have turned out to be real animals. People once believed in a cryptid called the kraken. It was said to pull ships underwater. Researchers now believe this animal was the giant squid.

alien – creature not from Earth
cryptid – creature whose existence has not been proven by science

MONSTER IN THE MOUNTAINS

The snowy Himalayas in Asia may hold a hairy secret. People have spotted an apelike creature called the yeti in the mountains for years. Some reports say the yeti has white fur. Others say its fur is dark. Many people think the yeti is a kind of ape that hasn't been discovered. Reports say the yeti stands 2.4 metres (8 feet) tall or more. It is said to weigh about 136 kilograms (300 pounds).

The word *yeti* comes from the **Sherpa** phrase "yet-teh". The word has many meanings, including "little manlike animal" and "animal of rocky places".

Sherpa – member of a group of Tibetan people living in the Himalayas in eastern Nepal; Sherpas are known for helping mountain climbers

A HAIRY BLOODSUCKER

Move over, Count Dracula. There's a new bloodsucking monster on the hunt – the chupacabra. According to legend, this doglike cryptid sucks the blood of small animals. It hunts in Central America and the southern United States. Reports say it has glowing eyes and long, sharp claws. A terrible smell follows wherever it goes. *Sceptics* say the chupacabra is a dog or coyote with a skin disease.

sceptic – person who questions things that other people believe in

The word *chupacabra* means "goat sucker" in Spanish.

A DEADLY DRAGON

According to *folklore*, a hideous dragon once lived in the River Wear in north-east England. Called the Lambton Worm, slimy skin covered its body. It had no legs or wings. Its breath killed anyone who smelled it. This monster snatched up animals and people with its sharp teeth. At night the dragon wrapped its huge body around a hill to sleep.

folklore – ideas or stories that are not true but that many people have heard

SWAMP BEAST

Beware of the swamps and
lakes of Australia. The bunyip is
said to call these waters home.
Reports about the creature's looks
vary. Some say it has the head of
an *emu* or dog with a hairy body.
The bunyip eats anyone who dares
to enter its watery home. But even
people on land aren't safe. At night
this monster leaves the water.
It gobbles up everyone in sight.

The *Aborigines* of Australia first described the bunyip. These people arrived in Australia about 50,000 years ago.

A BUNYIP OF ABORIGINAL LEGEND

emu – large, flightless Australian bird that runs fast
Aborigine – one of the native peoples of Australia whose ancestors lived there before Europeans arrived

15

BULL-HEADED MONSTER

The minotaur was one of the scariest monsters from ancient Greek *myths*. It had the head of a bull. Its body was human. This beast used razor-sharp teeth and horns to attack its *victims*.

The minotaur lived in a *labyrinth*. It hungered for only one thing – human flesh. Anyone caught in its mazelike home was eaten alive.

myth – story told by people in ancient times; myths often tried to explain natural events

victim – person who is hurt, killed or made to suffer

labyrinth – maze of winding passages

According to the myth, the Greek hero Theseus killed the minotaur.

THE FLYING HEAD

According to Malaysian folklore, a bloodsucking monster lives in plain sight. During the day the Penanggalan looks like a woman. But at night its head detaches from its body. Guts dangle from this monster's head as it flies around. It hungers for human blood.

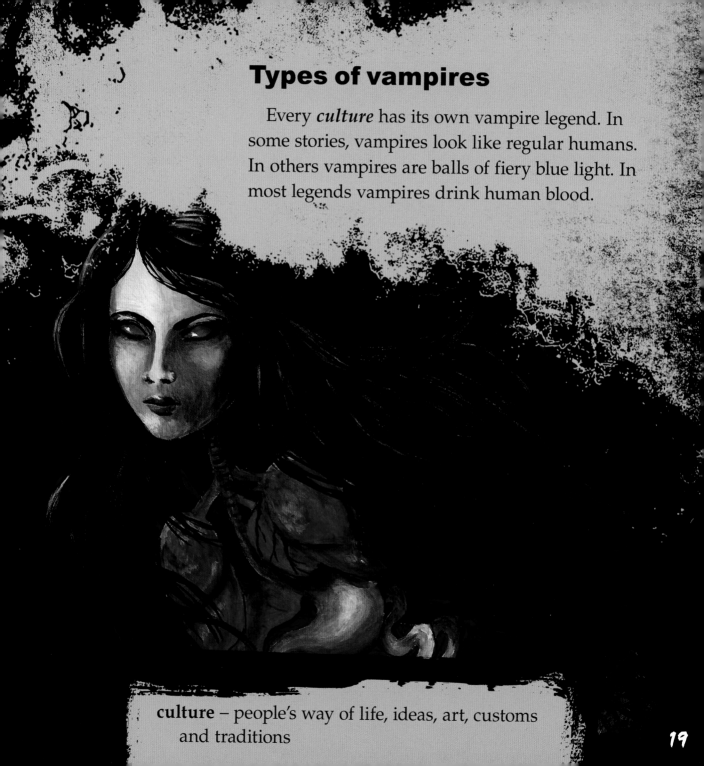

Types of vampires

Every *culture* has its own vampire legend. In some stories, vampires look like regular humans. In others vampires are balls of fiery blue light. In most legends vampires drink human blood.

culture – people's way of life, ideas, art, customs and traditions

A WATERY END

English folklore says the murky ponds of northern England hide a scary monster. A woman with green skin, hair and teeth hides beneath the surface. She is called Jenny Greenteeth. This monster waits for children to come near. She then uses her long arms and sharp nails to drag them to their doom.

The Jenny Greenteeth story isn't real. But some people think the yeti and other monsters might exist. Real or not, it's fun to tell stories about creepy monsters among us.

Jenny Greenteeth is sometimes called Wicked Jenny.

GLOSSARY

Aborigine   one of the native peoples of Australia whose ancestors lived there before Europeans arrived

alien   creature not from Earth

cryptid   creature whose existence has not been proven by science

culture   people's way of life, ideas, art, customs and traditions

emu   large, flightless Australian bird that runs fast

folklore   ideas or stories that are not true but that many people have heard

labyrinth   maze of winding passages

legendary   something based on a story handed down from earlier times; legends are often based on fact, but they may not be entirely true

myth   story told by people in ancient times; myths often tried to explain natural events

sceptic   person who questions things that other people believe in

Sherpa   member of a group of Tibetan people living in the Himalayas in eastern Nepal; Sherpas are known for helping mountain climbers

victim   person who is hurt, killed or made to suffer

READ MORE

Chupacabras! (Jr. Graphic Monster Stories), Steven Roberts (PowerKids Press, 2013)

Scooby-Doo! and the Truth Behind Vampires (Unmasking Monsters with Scooby-Doo!), Mark Weakland (Capstone, 2015)

The Unsolved Mystery of Bigfoot (Unexplained Mysteries), Michael Burgan (Capstone, 2013)

WEBSITES

Yeti Facts:
natgeotv.com/ca/hunt-for-the-abominable-snowman/facts

The Science Behind Bigfoot and Other Monsters:
news.nationalgeographic.com/news/2013/09/130907-cryptid-crytozoology-bigfoot-loch-yeti-monster-abominable-science

INDEX